J

Main

D1736852

COUNTRY PROFILES
PORTUGAL

BY GOLRIZ GOLKAR

BLASTOFF! DISCOVERY

BELLWETHER MEDIA • MINNEAPOLIS, MN

Blastoff! Discovery launches a new mission: reading to learn. Filled with facts and features, each book offers you an exciting new world to explore!

BLASTOFF! UNIVERSE

BLASTOFF! Beginners — GRADE K

BLASTOFF! READERS — GRADES 1-3

DISCOVERY — GRADE 4

This edition first published in 2021 by Bellwether Media, Inc.

No part of this publication may be reproduced in whole or in part without written permission of the publisher.
For information regarding permission, write to Bellwether Media, Inc.,
Attention: Permissions Department,
6012 Blue Circle Drive, Minnetonka, MN 55343.

Library of Congress Cataloging-in-Publication Data

Names: Golkar, Golriz, author.
Title: Portugal / by Golriz Golkar.
Description: Minneapolis, MN : Bellwether Media, Inc., 2021. |
    Series: Blastoff! Discovery: Country Profiles | Includes
    bibliographical references and index. | Audience: Ages 7-13 |
    Audience: Grades 4-6 | Summary: "Engaging images accompany
    information about Portugal. The combination of high-interest subject
    matter and narrative text is intended for students in grades
    3 through 8" Provided by publisher.
Identifiers: LCCN 2020001640 (print) | LCCN 2020001641 (ebook)
    | ISBN 9781644872567 (library binding) | ISBN
    9781681037196 (ebook)
Subjects: LCSH: Portugal–Juvenile literature.
Classification: LCC DP517 .G65 2021 (print) | LCC DP517 (ebook)
    | DDC 946.9–dc23
LC record available at https://lccn.loc.gov/2020001640
LC ebook record available at https://lccn.loc.gov/2020001641

Editor: Kieran Downs   Designer: Brittany McIntosh

Printed in the United States of America, North Mankato, MN.

TABLE OF CONTENTS

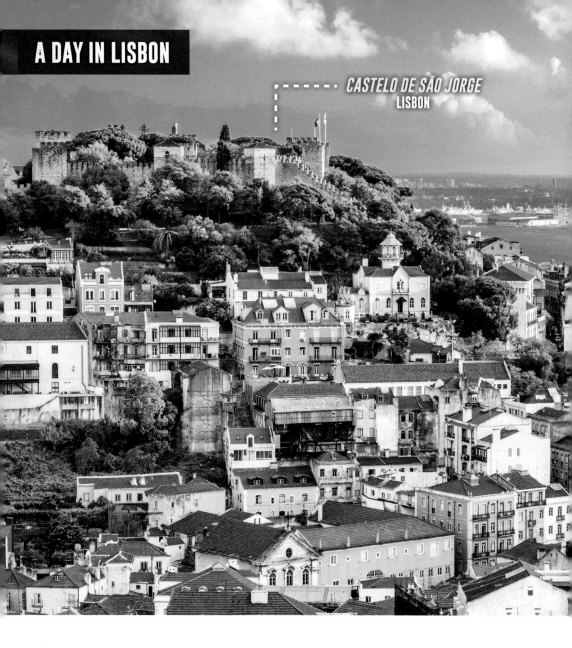

CASTELO DE SÃO JORGE
LISBON

   A family strolls down winding cobblestone streets after visiting the *Castelo de São Jorge*, or St. George's Castle, in Lisbon. The ancient castle towers above the city center. Next, the family enters the Alfama district, the oldest neighborhood in the city. Small restaurants serve local dishes such as *chouriço* sausage.

4

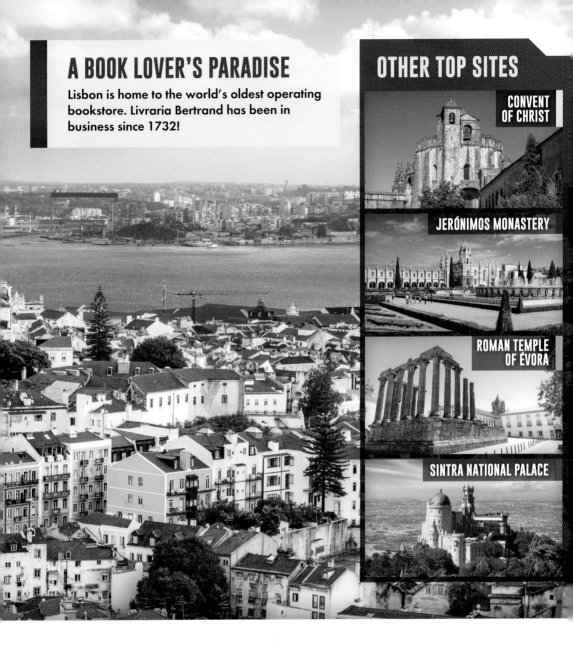

A BOOK LOVER'S PARADISE

Lisbon is home to the world's oldest operating bookstore. Livraria Bertrand has been in business since 1732!

OTHER TOP SITES

CONVENT OF CHRIST

JERÓNIMOS MONASTERY

ROMAN TEMPLE OF ÉVORA

SINTRA NATIONAL PALACE

The family takes in the sunset view from one of Lisbon's many viewpoints, known as *miradouros*. Eventually, they settle at a small restaurant. A lady sings a soft *fado* song. The music, landscape, and food offer just a taste of Portugal!

LOCATION

AZORES

MADEIRA

● - - - BRAGA

● - - - PORTO

PORTUGAL

AMADORA

★ - - - LISBON

ATLANTIC
OCEAN

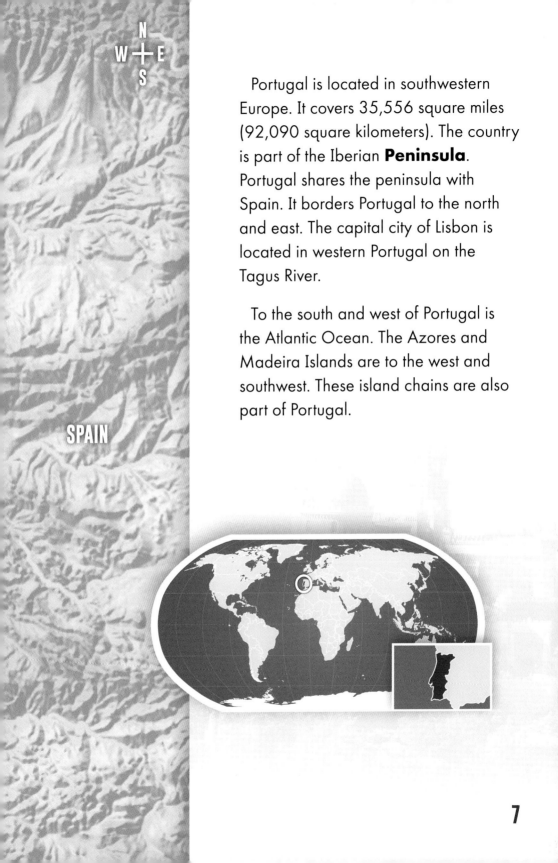

Portugal is located in southwestern Europe. It covers 35,556 square miles (92,090 square kilometers). The country is part of the Iberian **Peninsula**. Portugal shares the peninsula with Spain. It borders Portugal to the north and east. The capital city of Lisbon is located in western Portugal on the Tagus River.

To the south and west of Portugal is the Atlantic Ocean. The Azores and Madeira Islands are to the west and southwest. These island chains are also part of Portugal.

SPAIN

LANDSCAPE AND CLIMATE

Portugal features a variety of landscapes. The northern region is mostly mountainous. The Estrella Mountains are the highest in Portugal. The Tagus River flows west from central Portugal to the Atlantic Ocean. The southern region features rolling **plains**. Sandy beaches and rough cliffs line the southern coast. The Azores and Madeira Islands are known for their rough cliff coastlines and towering **volcanoes**.

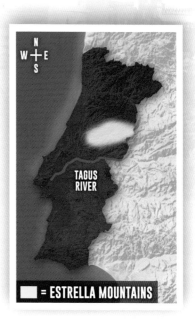

TAGUS RIVER

■ = ESTRELLA MOUNTAINS

A DIFFERENT KIND OF SWIMMING POOL

The town of Porto Moniz on Madeira has natural swimming pools formed from volcanic rock!

8

ESTRELLA
MOUNTAINS

LISBON

**Average
seasonal highs
and lows**

JANUARY
HIGH: 59 °F (15 °C)
LOW: 46 °F (8 °C)

APRIL
HIGH: 66 °F (19 °C)
LOW: 54 °F (12 °C)

JULY
HIGH: 82 °F (28 °C)
LOW: 64 °F (18 °C)

OCTOBER
HIGH: 72 °F (22 °C)
LOW: 59 °F (15 °C)

°F = degrees Fahrenheit
°C = degrees Celsius

The Atlantic Ocean gives Portugal a **temperate** climate. Summers are hot and dry, especially in the south. Winters are rainy and cool, especially in the north. Portugal's mountains may be covered in snow for months.

Portugal is home to many animals. All over the country, foxes hunt rabbits and Iberian hares. Wild pigs, goats, and deer roam the countryside. Wolves live in remote northern mountains.

Birdlife is very rich in Portugal. **Migratory** bird species such as the garden warbler and the European robin fly over the country. The Madeira Islands host several species of birds, including the Madeira laurel pigeon. The waters around the Madeira and Azores Islands are filled with wildlife. Sperm whales, stingrays, and bottlenose dolphins all make their homes there. The Atlantic waters of the **mainland** boast numerous kinds of fish, including the striped red mullet.

EUROPEAN ROBIN

STRIPED RED MULLET

RED FOX

RETURN OF THE LYNX

Iberian lynx once roamed all over Portugal. But their numbers have fallen. Today, there are only about 400 in the world. But efforts are being made to bring them back!

IBERIAN HARE

IBERIAN HARE

Life Span: around 1 year
Red List Status: least concern

Iberian hare range =

LEAST CONCERN	NEAR THREATENED	VULNERABLE	ENDANGERED	CRITICALLY ENDANGERED	EXTINCT IN THE WILD	EXTINCT
▲						

WHO ELSE SPEAKS PORTUGUESE?

Brazilians also speak Portuguese. Brazil is the only country in Latin America where Portuguese is the official language!

More than 10 million people live in Portugal. Most Portuguese have European backgrounds. Other major **ethnic** groups in Portugal include Brazilians, Han Chinese, and Roma. Some Portuguese are **immigrants** from Portugal's former colonies in Africa and Asia.

Almost all Portuguese people are Roman Catholic. A small number are Protestant, Jewish, or Muslim. Portuguese is the official language of the country. Nearly everyone speaks Portuguese as their first language. Mirandese is a **dialect** spoken by some people in northern parts of the country.

FAMOUS FACE

Name: Cristiano Ronaldo
Birthday: February 5, 1985
Hometown: Funchal, Madeira, Portugal
Famous for: Star soccer player, supporter of children's causes, and owner of the clothing and footwear brand CR7

SPEAK PORTUGUESE

ENGLISH	PORTUGUESE	HOW TO SAY IT
hello	olà	OH-lah
goodbye	tchau	CHOW
please	por favor	POUR fa-VOR
thank you	obrigado	oh-bree-GAH-doo
yes	sim	SEEM
no	não	NOW

CASCAIS

Most of the Portuguese population lives in **urban** areas. They live near the Atlantic coast in large cities such as Lisbon and Porto. Their homes are typically apartment buildings. People in **rural** Portugal may live in small villages or on farms. Many people live with relatives. Children often live with their parents until they are grown up. Grandparents may help raise children.

PORTO

A COLORFUL COUNTRY

Portuguese buildings are often covered in decorative tiles called *azulejos*. Some date back to the 16th century. They can be found on both the outside and inside of buildings.

LISBON

Portugal's cities are connected by a railroad system. This lets people travel across the country. In cities, people get around on the subway. Many have cars, too. Boat travel is common on the Douro River.

FADO
BAND

Music and dance are at the heart of Portuguese **culture**. Each region has its own musical styles. However, the fado style is celebrated throughout Portugal. Fado musicians sing about life's troubles. In Coimbra, fado is only performed by males. Lisbon fado is more popular. It may be sung by anyone.

In some regions, people wear **traditional** clothing for special events. In the Minho **province**, women wear red and white costumes with gold necklaces to weddings. Cattle farmers in the Alentejo region wear red and green stocking caps.

TRADITIONAL
MINHO CLOTHING

17

OLD SCHOOL

The University of Coimbra is one of the world's oldest operating universities. It was founded in 1290! The school was originally located in Lisbon before it was moved to Coimbra.

TOQUE AQUI

APALPÁRIO
TOUCH POOL

State schools are free for Portuguese children starting at age 3. Private schools are also available. School is required between the ages of 6 and 18. Children attend primary school for six years. Then they attend middle and high school for six years. Many students attend university after high school. Some attend specialized schools or military academies.

More than half of all Portuguese workers have **service jobs**. Many have jobs in **tourism**. Fishing is another major industry. Local specialties such as leather goods, cork, and tomato paste are also **manufactured** in Portugal.

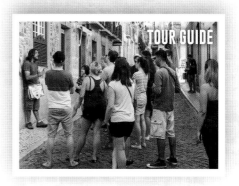

TOUR GUIDE

CORK FACTORY

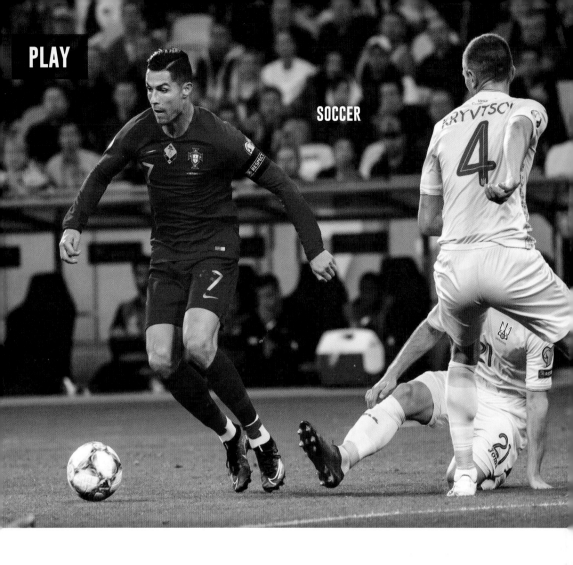

SOCCER

The most popular sport in Portugal is soccer. The Portuguese love supporting their national soccer team at games. Portuguese long-distance runners have won gold medals at the Olympic Games. Basketball is also very popular.

RUNNING

Portugal's coastal location and mild climate attract many beachgoers. The Algarve region is a popular beach destination in the summer. Sailing and surfing are popular ocean activities. The underwater canyons at Pelo Negro attract scuba divers. People of all ages love visiting national parks!

SURFING

PAINTED AZULEJO TILES

Portuguese buildings are often decorated with *azulejos*. They were originally designed with blue and white colors. Today, you can see tiles in many colors. Try making your own!

What You Need:
- white or solid colored tiles, or square pieces of construction paper
- paintbrushes
- acrylic paint, glitter paint, markers, crayons, or colored pencils
- stencils
- a permanent black marker

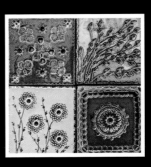

Instructions:
1. Draw a design on a tile or square piece of construction paper with the permanent marker. Use a stencil to make specific shapes.

2. Decorate your tile or paper using a pattern you like. You may use acrylic paint, glitter paint, markers, crayons, or colored pencils.

3. When the tile is complete, hang it with a hook, use it as a coaster, or pin it on a wall.

TOP SECRET RECIPE

Although the *pastéis de nata* is found all over Portugal, only three people in the world know the original recipe. The famous Pasteis de Belém pastry shop in Lisbon sells this version.

PASTEIS DE BELÉM

The Portuguese love having a pastry with espresso for breakfast. Desserts like *pastéis de nata*, or egg custard tart, are also found in Portugal's many pastry shops.

Fresh fish is commonly eaten all over Portugal. Cod is eaten grilled, baked, and deep-fried as fritters or cakes. *Bacalhau*, or salted cod, is the national dish. Pork and cured meats are popular in the Alentejo region. Sausage is a Lisbon favorite.

BACALHAU

FEIJOADA À TRANSMONTANA

A popular sausage stew is *feijoada à transmontana*, prepared with beans and cabbage. Rice is used in main dishes and desserts.

PORTUGUESE RICE PUDDING

Try making this tasty recipe with the help of an adult!

Ingredients:
1 cup short-grain rice
2 1/4 cups water for cooking rice
1/2 teaspoon salt for cooking rice
2 cups preheated milk
1 lemon rind, cut into long strips
cinnamon for decoration

Steps:
1. Boil the water, salt, and lemon rind in a medium-sized saucepan.
2. Reduce heat to low, cover, and let the water simmer for 15 minutes.
3. Remove the lemon rind with a slotted spoon.
4. Add the rice to the water and return to a boil. Then, reduce to a simmer and cook for about 10 minutes.
5. Slowly add the preheated milk to the rice, about 1/2 cup at a time. Let each portion of milk absorb before adding the next cup.
6. Stir the rice frequently over low heat for 25 to 30 minutes.
7. Pour the cooked rice into a serving dish. Sprinkle with cinnamon and chill before serving.

The Portuguese celebrate many holidays throughout the year. Lively music and colorful costumes take over the streets during Carnival in February. Freedom Day is observed on April 25 with parades and cultural events. It marks the day Portugal became a **democracy**.

In May and October, many Catholics travel to the holy **shrine** of Fatima. They pray and worship the Virgin Mary where she is said to have appeared many years ago. On Christmas Eve, many people decorate a **nativity** scene. Families enjoy salted cod and fried desserts for dinner. The Portuguese honor their culture all year long!

IT'S ALIVE!

The largest moving nativity scene in the world was hosted in Portugal in 2012. It featured 7,000 moving figurines!

CARNIVAL

1494
The Treaty of Tordesillas settles a dispute between Spain and Portugal over newly discovered lands, giving Portugal land east of the Cape Verde Islands

AROUND 1000 BCE
Celtic people settle in what is now modern-day Portugal

1755
A major earthquake centered near Lisbon destroys the city

1139 CE
The Kingdom of Portugal is formed

1415
Henry the Navigator orders several expeditions to Africa, starting Portugal's colonial empire

1498
Portuguese explorer Vasco da Gama reaches India by sea, opening a route for trade with Europe

1932

Antonio de Oliveira Salazar becomes prime minister, starting 42 years of dictators ruling Portugal

2016

Marcelo Rebelo de Sousa is elected president, promising to restore stability to the Portuguese government

1974

The peaceful Carnation Revolution establishes a democratic government in Portugal, granting independence to Portugal's African colonies

2011

Portugal receives money from the European Union to help with debt and unemployment

PORTUGAL FACTS

Official Name: Portuguese Republic

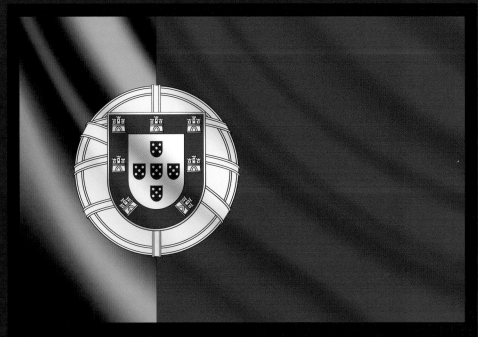

Flag of Portugal: The Portuguese flag bears two vertical bands. The smaller green band represents hope. The larger red band represents the blood of those who defend the country. In the middle of the two bands is the Portuguese coat of arms. It contains symbols showing Portugal's faith, history, and role in the world.

Area: 35,556 square miles
(92,090 square kilometers)

Capital City: Lisbon

Important Cities: Porto, Amadora, Braga

Population:
10,302,674 (July 2020)

WHERE PEOPLE LIVE

COUNTRYSIDE
33.7%

CITY
66.3%

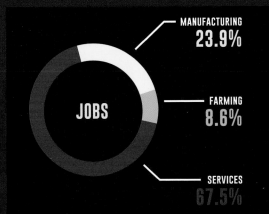

MANUFACTURING
23.9%

JOBS

FARMING
8.6%

SERVICES
67.5%

Main Exports:

chemicals

leather

foods

wood products

National Holiday:
Portugal Day (June 10)

Main Language:
Portuguese

Form of Government:
semi-presidential republic

Title for Country Leaders:
president (chief of state),
prime minister (head of government)

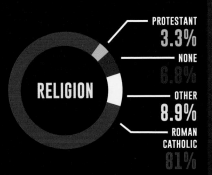

RELIGION

PROTESTANT
3.3%

NONE
6.8%

OTHER
8.9%

ROMAN CATHOLIC
81%

Unit of Money:
Euro

GLOSSARY

culture—the beliefs, arts, and ways of life in a place or society

democracy—a government run by the people

dialect—a local way of speaking a particular language

ethnic—related to a group of people who share customs and an identity

immigrants—people who move to a new country

mainland—a continent or main part of a continent

manufactured—produced, often with machines

migratory—referring to animals that travel from one place to another, often with the seasons

nativity—the birth of Jesus Christ

peninsula—a section of land that extends out from a larger piece of land and is almost completely surrounded by water

plains—large areas of flat land

province—an area within a country; provinces follow all the laws of the country and make some of their own laws.

rural—related to the countryside

service jobs—jobs that perform tasks for people or businesses

shrine—a place thought to be holy because of its connections with someone or something holy

temperate—associated with a mild climate that does not have extreme heat or cold

tourism—the business of people traveling to visit other places

traditional—related to customs, ideas, or beliefs handed down from one generation to the next

urban—related to cities and city life

volcanoes—holes in the earth; when volcanoes erupt, hot ash, gas, or melted rock called lava shoots out.

TO LEARN MORE

AT THE LIBRARY

Birdoff, Ariel Factor. *Countries We Come From: Portugal.* New York, N.Y.: Bearport Publishing, 2019.

Carvalho, Sérgio Luís de. *A Children's History of Portugal.* North Dartmouth, Mass.: Tagus Press, 2017.

Rechner, Amy. *Spain.* Minneapolis, Minn.: Bellwether Media, 2019.

ON THE WEB

FACTSURFER

Factsurfer.com gives you a safe, fun way to find more information.

1. Go to www.factsurfer.com.

2. Enter "Portugal" into the search box and click Q.

3. Select your book cover to see a list of related content.

INDEX